A Search For Enlightenment In An Age Of Indoctrination

Implementing Meta Cognitive Thinking

A Search For Enlightenment In An Age Of Indoctrination

Implementing Meta Cognitive Thinking

Dr. Rudy Magnan

To order additional copies of this book, contact:
Xlibris
844-714-8691
www.Xlibris.com
Orders@Xlibris.com
852411

Contents

PREFACE

HUMANS HAVE ALWAYS SOUGHT TO figure out their existence and the unknown forces that impact their survival. This challenge continues to impact their daily lives. Today humans still are searching for enlightenment and meaning maybe as never before because they suffer from an 'information anxiety', the result of a continuous information bombardment from the mass media and the powerful social media to which they seem addicted.

Human beings are unable to confront these forces because their cognitive development is in decline due to a failed educational system that makes passive learners filled with information. Consequently, they lack the mental processing skills necessary for creating a 'proactive info processing' platform. In the past, humans depended on developing their perceptual skills; they allowed them to add new insights and ideas to their 'web of understanding'. This mental development was critical to creating their unique body of knowledge whereby their members interacted. This learning was communicated for the education of new generations.

Today, current segments of society seem to be focused on letting computers and new tech gadgets do our thinking. Young people are attracted to these inventions which seem to manipulate their perceptions and behavior. We seem to have ignored the ideas and insights of great creative thinkers.

I have researched the perceptual thinking of a few of these individuals whose contributions seem dismissed or ignored. I believe that we have much to learn from their ideas and insights if only to prioritize the perceptual skills they developed.

I believe that these creative thinkers identified an incredible potential of the mind to view reality with a different set of spectacles. Leonardo da Vinci's motto was to "Sapere a Vedere'. He often challenged existing perceptions and knowledge to open his mind to new insights and information. He developed an insatiable curiosity in discovering new realities.

Castaneda believed that the mind had this ability to attain practical wisdom from the Shamans of Ancient Mexico. This involved observing energy to turn it into sensory energy in the universe as a tool to alter the illusions of the finality in this one world. Humans can sense the multiple worlds with this perception, and they can act accordingly. The concept may seem odd, but it provides an alternative way of thinking analogous to the beliefs and practices of Leonardo da Vinci.

The third creative thinker is Dr. Edward de Bono with whom I collaborated in promoting his 'Lateral Thinking'. He placed great emphasis on challenging existing notions by utilizing illogical ways of creating solutions or by solving complicated problems.

He emphasized the need to raise the quality of our thinking which often becomes trapped in an intelligence trap that very intelligent people find themselves.

They seek to only defend their point of view, never exploring other viewpoints. Consequently, they can never develop creative thinking.

They fail to realize that thinking is our most important natural resource when trying to solve complicated problems.

All three of these individuals sought to implement the adage "think outside the box". To accomplish this task, they sought to change our perceptions of our mental potential. They looked to tap into a reservoir of mental energy that would stimulate our minds toward a new personal enlightenment.

Once we arrive at this heightened awareness, we become aware of the power of this new mental processing energy. We cannot be focused on using only learned information to become creative thinkers. The key that opens the door to this creative reservoir of new ideas occurs when we develop new perceptual processing skills which the three creative thinkers proposed. This manuscript is written in my belief that this should be our focus in our current search for enlightenment.

INTRODUCTION

I AM CONVINCED THAT THERE IS more to explore and understand if we stimulate and train our minds 'to think outside the box'. There is a universe of ideas and insights to discover if we make a conscious effort to seek out this unexplored universe that is filled with incredible information and data. Yet, if we continue to only depend on current tech gadgets, we will fail to expand our perception. It is critical to realize the power of the mind to open our thinking to new ways of achieving a new creative mental behavior.

Past civilizations believed that developing this Third Eye or sixth sense opened their consciousness to become enlightened with new knowledge. This Third Eye was considered "the eye of knowledge". In the past centuries, people were obliged to use their minds to figure out how to think outside the box. They developed their perceptual abilities to make new gadgets, new ways of living, new ways of getting around, new ways of communication. Many items were recycled for use another day. Few items were discarded, so there was a continuous use of creative thinking ability to meet their everyday challenges.

In our current era of abundance, we seem to have lost this creative sixth sense. We live in 'a throw -away society'. Creative thinking skills are ignored or in decline in our school curriculum. Many students graduating have not achieved basic levels of proficiency in math, science, and reading.

Many demonstrate an inability to mentally figure simple money computations. Many college graduates have difficulty in making decisions in the workplace. The alarm has sounded in many urban areas because we have generations of young people who seem unable to deal with the many challenges they face in this complex, changing social environment. It is important that we now realize the need to introduce creative thinking skills. It is time to become aware of the power of the mind with the use of our 'sixth sense'.

Da Vinci pursued his observations, always looking to identify new details that were not seen. He spent countless hours observing and documenting the dynamics of birds in flight. He dissected many human corpses to understand their unique designs and operating systems. In his painting of the Last Supper, he studied the effect light at different times of the day would have on the fresco wall. He also had an insatiable curiosity for depicting different images of religious figures in his many paintings. His creative thinking produced futuristic designs of parachutes, airplanes, submarines, bicycles, musical instruments, military weaponry, etc.

As one of the great Renaissance thinkers, da Vinci may have developed this sixth sense that helps to explain his genius creative abilities. He often expressed the belief that when you change the way you look at things, the things you look at change, implying that you see everything in a different way. New insights, new ideas, new knowledge emerges. This experience triggers the mind to search and learn more. This desire pushes the mind to function in a visual dimension.

The mind using this creative way of perceiving accumulates large amounts of new visual data. But it seems unnatural for how our two eyes process observed phenomena.

There must be another brain mechanism that can explain this way of mental capacity to utilize their third eye are sometimes known as seers. These third eye abilities in the past were often associated with precognition, clairvoyance, visions. Hindus place a "tilaka" between the eyebrows to represent their third eye. Buddhists regard the third eye as the eye of consciousness from which enlightenment beyond one's physical sight is achieved. Taoism teaches that the third eye is called the mind's eye. It is situated between the two physical eyes.

This third eye is considered one of the main energy centers of the body forming part of the main meridian. This meridian separates the right and left hemispheres of the body. Other theories include the one suggested by H.P. Blavatsky that the third eye is in fact the partially dormant pineal gland which resides between both hemispheres of the brain. C. W. Leadbeater theorized that the third eye is capable of microscopic vision capable of observing quirks. It is also believed that reptiles and amphibians send light through a third parietal eye believed associated with the pineal gland which serves to aid in navigation and to regulate circadian rhythms since this gland can sense the polarization of light. In the Indian spiritual traditions, the third eye opens one's mind to new inner realms and to higher consciousness. It is part of the sixth chakra. In spiritual terms it symbolizes a state of enlightenment.

The Chakras are thought to be wheel-like energy centers distributed throughout the body that affect perception and well-being. The third eye chakra is believed to be connected to intuition, imagination, concentration, clarity and to a universal connection.

The third eye has significant meaning in America. It was inserted on the back of our dollar bill. It symbolizes the eye of Providence, an "all seeing" God. The eye is enclosed in a triangle surrounded by rays of light. It is meant to represent a Divine Providence overlooking our humanity. America was founded on Christian beliefs.

Our founding fathers' thinking and perception of our humanity were manifested in our Declaration of Independence. They believed that our God given humanity included certain inalienable rights of life, liberty, and the pursuit of happiness. These ideas were initially espoused in the late sixteen century by French Philosophers Voltaire and Montesquieu in what became the Age of Enlightenment.

The American philosopher John Locke was one of the most influential Enlightenment thinkers whose writings contributed to the development of the concepts of social contact and natural rights.

Considering all these historical associations with this third eye, I was convinced that this concept was worth developing, especially today when we are living and working in a new Creative Paradigm where higher-level perceptual processing is required.

It is an idea that has evolved over centuries in different world regions, in different religious belief systems and in the advancement of the human condition.

In history the Third Eye was believed to be the gateway to consciousness. It was also known as the 'inner eye' a mystical concept referred as the 'ajne chakra." The use of this ability was also associated with clairvoyance, precognition and even out of body experiences. Both in Hindu and Buddhis traditions, it was the symbol of enlightenment. It was believed to be the 'eye of knowledge'.

Yet, this idea now seems ignored. We are living in a new creative paradigm which demands not only greater knowledge but also greater ability to use information to find what is not apparent in our minds. As inhabitants of this planet earth, we have learned to describe what we see around us through the language we use to label the things we see. Technological advances in photography show a different visual reality that is far more elaborate and interesting than what we see. There are many scientific discoveries that reveal an 'intelligent design' behind all the plants, trees, and living things around us. Our own physical bodies undergo an incredible physical transformation. Our skin, our bones, and our organs change but we can't see it happening. We see our hair and nails grow but do not see the incredible complex cellular operating system that keeps us alive and healthy.

We find it difficult to change our established perception which manipulates how we process information. This mental process is critical in relation to how we understand and attain meaning from the things we see. We are born with two eyes and an intelligent creative brain that collaborates to produce awareness but also leads to discoveries of things that were not previously apparent.

CHAPTER ONE

Sixth Sense – Third Eye Discoveries

WHILE WE REMAIN CONVINCED THAT what we perceive and understand defines our intelligence, we need to think outside of our intelligence box. There is a surprising alternative explanation that opens the mind to new insights. It involves understanding that we likely possess a sixth sense that we ignore that generates new discoveries of ideas and information that were not obvious in our perceptions.

The mental processing of information can be upgraded with a reliance on a new operating concept known as the 'third eye'. This idea involves looking beyond the obvious reality we observe in our surrounding environment. Recent research about intelligent operating systems in nature indicates that they have certain design features and behavior that has a genius quality. Jane Benyus has documented this in her book titled 'MIMICRY'. We have much to learn from nature's R/D which has operated over centuries perfecting its 'intelligent design'.

The following examples demonstrate how man has applied these discoveries to solving problems or improving existing systems.

Consider how Biomimicry was applied in different fields, demonstrating that nature had tackled similar challenges.

Human need: Builders want a cheaper means of cooling a large building.

Nature's example: Certain African termite mounds must maintain a constant temperature of 87 degrees Celsius (189 degrees Fahrenheit) in order for the fungus crop to survive. To achieve this, they construct air vents that constantly move air throughout the mound, cooling or heating it to the same temperature as the mound itself.

Biomimetic Solution: Architects and engineers are building several large office complexes that mimic the termite approach to temperature control.

Human need: Auto manufacturers want to develop an anti-collision system.

Nature's example: Locusts avoid running into each other in swarms by using highly evolved eyes that allow these insects to see in several directions simultaneously.

Biomimetic solution: Automobile designers mimicked the locusts' vision when developing sensors that detect movement directly surrounding a car and warn drivers of impending crashes.

Human need: Chemical companies want a self-cleaning coat of paint.

Nature's example: Lotus plants must keep the surfaces of their leaves clean, despite living in muddy ponds and swamps. The leaves' tiny ridges and bumps keep water droplets from spreading across the surface. As a result, the water beads slide away, carrying particles of dirt with it.

Biomimetic solution: Developers have applied this lotus effect to paint. When the paint dries, tiny bumps remain on the surface that help water droplets remove dirt.

Human need: Health workers want a way to store vaccines with refrigeration.

Nature's example: The African resurrection plant completely dries out during yearly droughts and then revives itself when the rains return. The plants contain a polyphenol that protects against cell membrane damage during dehydration.

The study of nature's intelligent design and function could be the basis for expanding your thinking, image using and imagined 'third eye' which allows you to begin to study nature's 'research and development' efforts that have allowed nature to survive serious problems and challenges over the centuries. Nature has shown an incredible ability to adapt and transform itself under all kinds of adverse conditions. Some of our commercial initiatives and ventures have failed due to our inability to make the necessary creative transformations in our workforce.

This can be explained by a failure to develop an imagined 'third eye' to view and identify key changes, conditions, and trends. Many entrepreneurs tend to avoid thinking creatively about what is really happening in their routine operations. If they included 'creative thinking' skills as part of their management culture, that would help them become proactive instead of being reactive when faced with unexpected events and challenges.

We only recently have discovered that we are interlinked with nature as a link in a remarkable ecosystem. Our future survival as a species will depend on how we learn to apply this 'intelligent design' to how we live our lives and to how we relate to each other as human beings. We need to rethink the ideas and values that define our civility and culture. Benyus suggests looking more to nature for sustainable ways to produce quality materials and processes. She outlines nature's seven "rules" below, source: http://www.interfacesustainability.com/mimicry. html". Following them might lead to ways we could engineer a more sustainable way of life for humans.

- Nature runs on sunlight.
- Nature uses only the energy it needs.
- Nature fits form to function.
- Nature recycles everything.
- Nature rewards cooperation.
- Nature banks on diversity.
- Nature demands local expertise.
- Nature curbs excesses from within.
- Nature taps the power of limits.

We need to become "uniceptive", capable of understanding multiple "mind sets" (multiple systems of thinking). This flexibility will also allow us to increase our understanding and mental flexibility. Ackoff offers a significant insight:

Progress comes as much from creative reorganization of what we already know as from the discovery of new things. Einstein's contribution to physics was organizational. All the facts available to him were available to others. In the last two decades, science itself has undergone extensive reorganization with the emergence of many new "interdisciplines" such as cybernetics, operations research, communication sciences, and general systems. A filing system can always be reorganized without changing its content but doing so may increase our access to, and understanding of, that content. Therefore, we should not imbed our current ways of classifying knowledge in students' minds as fixed categories. They should be encouraged to organize their learning in ways that best serve them, not us. This new perspective should motivate us to challenge the existing model and to make the needed changes in our current education system.

"We live in an incredible design environment where there is a continuous mathematical transformation of living species as they are added, multiplied, divided, and subtracted".

Dr. Rudy Magnan "Mindsight"

But have we lost the search for human understanding that is part of our creative destiny in this new millennium? We continue to look at nature in all its cosmetic manifestations.

We fail to appreciate its intricate complexity and transformations that often hold us in awe during the seasonal changes that take place during the year. These visual physical changes operate within a remarkable intelligent 'flow of energy' involving chemical, biological, mechanical elements that have been perfected over centuries of trial and error.

If we reflect upon this multifaceted 'flow of energy', we also discover a relevant and meaningful notion. Nature possesses hidden secrets, and we have an opportunity to discover them. This experience can open our minds. The closer we look at some of the creatures in our physical environment, the more we begin to observe another reality with a kind of 'third eye'. For example, at the beginning of the 1980's, scientist Irene Pepperberg studied the behavior of an African grey parrot in order to show that he had certain intellectual capabilities rivaling that of primates. Before his death, this parrot had mastered a vocabulary of objects of various colors and materials and physically identify which were of a certain type with remarkable accuracy. He could use numbers to answer questions about addition. He also demonstrated a knowledge of abstract concepts as well as an ability to sound out words like 'nut' as a child would. Alex showed an ability to comprehend words and respond with a certain cogency, intelligence. The night before he died, he repeated his daily refrain "You be good, see you tomorrow, I love you".

Scientists initially believed that birds have no brains, but recent research shows otherwise. Birds have brains very different from ours. Some birds have large brains for their body size. They possess remarkable airborne skills that at times seem to defy gravity as they hover, dive, soar for days, migrate thousands of miles and can maneuver their flights in tight spaces. Birds can hide 30,000 seeds over dozens of miles and remember several months later where they put them. Mockingbirds and thrashers can store 200-2,000 different songs in a brain that is much smaller than ours.

Birds according to Jennifer Ackerman author of the 'Genius of Birds' shows research that demonstrates birds' unique genius abilities that seem unbelievable. They can deceive, manipulate, eavesdrop, offer gifts, blackmail others, and even alert other birds of dangers. What seems extraordinary is an ability to summon other witnesses to the passing of another bird and even grieve their death. All of these traits and abilities should motivate us to rethink our established notion of the meaning of intelligence.

CHAPTER TWO

Sixth Sense Scientific Discoveries

THERE ARE MANY EXAMPLES OF sudden discoveries that were made when the researcher sought to identify an unusual result that was unexpected. Alexander Fleming in 1928 was halfway through his experiment with bacteria when upon his return from vacation, he realized he had left thirty petri dishes in the lab sink. He discovered that the bacteria had grown all over the plate except for an area where mold had formed. This discovery led to the creation of penicillin. In the year 1844, nitrous oxide was strictly a party toy since it made people laugh like hyenas. A friend of dentist Horace Wells had taken too much of the gas, had fallen gashing his leg but never realized he had injured himself. Horace Wells was able to experiment with what was an early form of Anesthesia.

Another example of accidental inventions occurred when a Raytheon engineer in 1946 was looking for other uses for magnetron which generated microwaves for radar systems. One day as he was standing next to the device, he suddenly felt his chocolate bar in his pocket had melted. This discovery led to the invention of the microwave oven.

There is one last interesting invention made by Thomas Adams who was unsuccessful in testing the sap of a South American tree to find a substitute for rubber. One day he popped a piece of this in his mouth and liked it. This led to the production of chiclets chewing gum. We fail to realize that discoveries like those cited happened unexpectedly when the person doing the research suddenly opens his mind with a set of creative spectacles to focus on a new perception that leads to an invention. We don't realize that we live in a mathematically designed universe that creates a very intelligently organized environment. Yet, we seem incapable of understanding its relevant ramifications. However, I believe that there is a new virtual eye identified and used in the past that can reawaken our senses to visualize in an innovative way. This choice requires challenging our traditional ways of perception and thinking. We think and feel through the words we hear and see. This method of mental processing limits our powerful creative mind that seeks to help us make sense of the world. Our minds can process many more visual images than the many words we use. Consequently, it is imperative that we develop visual processing skills that develop higher level cognitive functioning.

We live and work in a new creative paradigm where creative ideas are the currency of the future. But operating successfully in this new paradigm requires new visual awareness skills to change the established mindset we use to operate and live in our physical surroundings.

CHAPTER THREE
CREATIVE DISCOVERIES
OF THE RENAISSANCE

MANY GREAT THINKERS HAVE EXPRESSED a belief that this ability can be developed. This idea is fundamental in understanding the genius mental abilities of Leonardo da Vinci. He believed that all knowledge originates within our perceptual ability. I believe that da Vinci discovered that "real intelligence" exists outside the mind. It is attainable if we challenge our established mindset and if we observe the surrounding 'intelligent design' in nature. He stressed the importance of "SAPER A VEDERE". This activity required changing the way you see things in order to open your mind to discovering new intelligent designs and concepts.

During the Renaissance period there was a rebirth of learning. It was a period where emerging thinkers and artists sought to challenge established artistic images. They were successful in creating new visual images of religious figures. He transformed the fixed images of the human figure into a more human image. Their efforts redefined and personalized an outmoded human depiction.

These innovative creative thinkers sought to explore new continents. They created new inventions, new artistic designs, new interest in new scientific endeavors. Their efforts had an immense impact on the creative development of society. It opened the medieval minds to more realistic ways of perceiving their figurative world. It ushered in new understandings and insights into things that were not previously obvious. It was truly a rebirth of learning.

I believe that innovators like Leonardo da Vinci had developed a creative mind using his 'virtual Third Eye' to challenge existing notions to attain new knowledge. Da Vinci's insatiable curiosity provoked a continuous interest in learning about all kinds of phenomena including the flight of birds, the human body's circulation, the mathematical measurements of trees and plants, and the unique physical designs of plants. Da Vinci also used this skill to design many innovative military weapons and fortifications.

One of the traits of a genius mind is the ability or skill to calculate proportions in different physical dimensions. Leonardo da Vinci developed this skill to figure out the design and function of whatever was under investigation. This awareness of spatial relationships was enhanced by his artistic depictions shown in his notebooks which were filled with continuous sketches and drawings. His creative mind quickly developed an ability to calculate distances, shapes and designs. This information was transmitted telepathically through his arms to his fingertips which effectively illustrated the ideas and designs he extracted.

Da Vinci believed that drawing is a scientific and superior demonstrative instrument far superior to the word. Drawings achieve perfection over what a writer faces in his oral discourse. This figurative discourse alternated his oral discourse resulting in fragmented thoughts alongside the thousands of unrelated notes.

As mentioned previously, Da Vinci was fascinated with different designs he studied and their respective function. He possessed an incredible visual ability that was demonstrated in the detailed notations in many of his codex. Where we see physical objects, his mind saw these objects in the particular linear designs. It is obvious he saw things through another visual dimension. This perspective allowed him to extract new insights, new creative possibilities that other scientists could not envision. He continued his practice of observing and documenting new details. This continuous mental processing transformed his mind resulting in genius abilities that produced innovative design and depictions in the painting of the Mona Lisa, the Last Supper.

His anatomical analysis of the human body made it possible to rediscover how the bodies' mechanics correspond to emotion according to the exact muscular movements. Here, as in other places, Da Vinci seems to value the importance of perception and the need for balance so that every muscle varies in volume according to whether or not it is in motion.

Da Vinci was continuously curious to figure out nature's inner operations. He spent considerable time observing phenomena in order to better understand what he saw. Da Vinci would observe a bird's physical flying skills from initial take-off during flight and he watched as they corrected their approach to a landing on a tree or on different physical objects. He must have wondered how they could figure out distances or spaces to adjust their landing speed. He soon realized that these creatures possessed a certain form of intelligence because they rarely made mistakes in their landing approach. He rarely saw birds crash into each other as they flew in formations over large distances. Da Vinci was able to quantum leap in his understanding of the natural environment around him. He was capable of exacting the maximum suggestive qualities freely expressed, producing extraordinary painting with a vision of perpetual action. His method is representative in hundreds of drawings. In this illustration previously mentioned, he portrays the head of a horse with fiercely upturned nostrils alongside the head of a roaring lion and the face of a screaming man. All three images create a very compelling sequence of "photograms". The result is that the drawings become more expressive and more intelligible than similar literal descriptions.

The key parts of visual thinking process include the eye, the brain, the hand and capability to modify the information that is being processed through the communication loop.

One of the traits of an analytical mind is the ability or skill to calculate proportions in different physical dimensions. Leonardo da Vinci developed this skill in order to figure out the design and function of whatever he was investigating. There was, I believe, a fascination with the different designs he studied and their respective function. He possessed an incredible skill to make detailed notation of what he saw. Where we see physical objects like trees, his mind saw things through another scientific dimension. This perspective allowed him to extract new insights, new creative possibilities that other scientists could not envision. He carefully recorded all his observations and continued to add new details that were not previously obvious. This continuous mental processing transformed his mental processing ability to document what previously was not understood.

The study of nature leads us to a realization of a Divine mind. The imitation of nature impacts the mind of the painter, the creative character of this divine mind. Da Vinci was always fascinated by the intelligent design in nature. He studied nature as if he were a pupil who wants to discover the secrets of nature in order to compete with this divinity in inventing and painting pictures that pulsate with life even in the machines and devices he produced where inert material comes alive.

Observational Skills as the Key to Receiving New Patterns of Recognition

If we take a closer look at nature, we see that it is also full of patterns, symmetry and order. Some creatures are almost perfectly symmetrical like a sea star and other echinoderms with identical limbs. Of all the 2,000 species of sea stars living in the ocean, most have five arms. Beyond the animal world, the snowflake is perhaps one of the best-known icons of symmetry formed from water crystals when water solidifies into crystals under certain conditions.

"The cerebral cortex which accounts for 80 percent of the human brain is composed of a highly repetitive structure, allowing humans to create arbitrating complex structure of ideas". ~David Shenk~

We seem to assume that intelligence is the result of our evolved mental operacy. We identify and label people as intelligent based on their ability to solve problems and deal with difficult challenges. Yet some of these individuals get caught in an "intelligent trap" because they tend to use their intelligence to defend their point of view. This confines their thinking to an established mind-set where they are unable to observe other points of view, possibilities, etc. This inability to look beyond the obvious is a perceptual problem that can be remedied by looking beyond the obvious or by viewing existing data with another set of spectacles.

"Logic is a tool invested for certain uses. It is not the way we deal with reality most of the time despite our conditioning".

As thinkers, we are consciously and unconsciously searching for meaning and identity. The goal of our information search is to create a web of meaning and understanding of "how things fit together." In this search, we are in the state of continuous mental activity in thinking out, in sorting out, and figuring out. Imagine for a moment that we are virtually orbiting in a "universe of ideas and concepts," organizing and reorganizing information on a daily basis. Those of us who have an insatiable appetite know more and to figure out more can do so by developing higher thinking processes. Da Vinci, (How to Think Like Leonardo) believed, as stated previously, that dealing with ambiguity and uncertainty was one of the first steps to achieve clarity and to finding the truth, "knowing how to see", looking beyond the obvious can sharpen your senses to improve your mind. There was a period of reflection on the arts in the second quarter of the 15th century. This enabled Da Vinci to formulate concepts, precise guidelines in matters related to painting but also to sculpture, architecture, etc.

Leonardo da Vinci believed basic understanding involved the developing of multiple points of view and that subsequent analyses of them led to complete and true knowledge. In designing the bicycle, he considered the opinions of the individuals sponsoring the prototype for production, the consumers who would purchase it, and the municipalities where the bicycles would be used. These multiple points of view increased his understanding and awareness of the required objectives that needed to be satisfied by his bicycle. His multiple considerations raised the quality of his thinking and represented an important step in the creative design process.

Da Vinci was continuously challenging the accepted point of view which probably maintained that sketching the three images on the same page made little sense, but in retrospect, considering the recent discoveries of the brain's most powerful mechanism (pattern recognition) in the neurosciences, it is likely that Da Vinci was implementing this powerful processing skill. As he developed this high-level ability, he sought to devote his curiosity to make new connections in his scientific pursuits but also in his continuous observations of all the intelligent designs within the natural world. He became fascinated by the wealth of new knowledge that could be discovered and applied using his new ability. During his lifetime, he made over six thousand entries in his notebooks which show an intelligence far advanced thinking even during the Renaissance period. He firmly believed that this ability could be developed. He suggested that it had to do with how we perceived what we saw. He saw things with a set of "creative spectacles". If we changed the way we viewed things, the things we viewed would change.

Another excellent example is evident in the invention of the fastener by George de Mestral in the 1940s. He and his dog brushed up against a bush that had burrs that stuck to his dog and his clothing and thereby created a problem because they were difficult to remove. Upon viewing the burrs under a microscope, he discovered hundreds of small hooks on each burr that would snag on to anything touching it.

Charles Darwin advanced his theory on evolution by focusing on an image of a tree to reorganize his thoughts in documenting his research. This allowed him to gather new insights by pulling in unrelated information. Each of these graphic representations was meaningful in his search for what was not known about evolution.

David Hawkins in his publication *Power vs. Force* provides us with some insights as to why we wrestle with this process of knowing.

Although we ascribe our actions to reason, man in fact operates primarily out of pattern of recognition, the logical arrangement of data serves mainly to enhance a pattern of recognition system that then become "truth." But nothing is ever true except under the circumstances and then only from a particular viewpoint, characteristically unstated.

Leonardo da Vinci became convinced that all knowledge begins with the use of a different set of spectacles to view and understand nature's secret designs. He began to develop this elevated perception as a child living on a farm. He soon became fascinated by the intelligent design in the natural things around the farm. He sought to learn more about the beautiful natural designs. With an ever-growing insatiable curiosity, he set out to observe and document the movements of natural phenomena.

It is apparent that we have lost interest in further exploration of these intelligent designs. It may be due to the development of words and not visual designs to describe what we see.

CHAPTER FOUR

THIRD EYE AS A PRIORITY FOR MENTAL GROWTH

TODAY WE CAN INITIATE A renewed interest in this concept known as the 'Third Eye' because now our technology operates as an analogous virtual 'Third Eye' using highly sophisticated optical instruments to study what was not apparent to the human eye. For example, a study of the 2,000 species of sea stars living in the ocean has documented that most have five arms. In addition, recent scientific research of snowflakes has concluded that every snowflake has a different design. Furthermore, the Japanese study has found that as a group, snowflakes exemplify nature's symmetry formed from water crystals that solidify according to climatic conditions.

Our failure to develop a virtual 'Third Eye' is due to the fact that younger generations have become too dependent on technological instruments and gadgets to figure things out. In this new millennium, creative thinking is not a priority mental skill in education. Its importance has diminished over time. This skill is necessary to succeed in this new creative economy where new ideas are the currency of the future. Yet, graduating college students need to develop survival mental skills. In a recent Harvard report on the skills necessary to succeed in the future included the ability to think creatively to discover what is not known in making a decision or in pursuing a project.

Considering all these factors, I became interested in developing this concept of a virtual 'Third Eye' because of its relevance in the past as a creative mind tool. Also because of recent discoveries by neuroscientists of the mind's powerful mechanism known as 'pattern recognition' that decides how we develop higher level understanding. This discovery increased my interest in research to see how this brain mechanism could lead to formulating a virtual platform where this 'Third Eye' ability could alter our perception and provoke our mind to develop creative thinking.

For example, we live in a physical reality that remains unexplored due to the fact that we recognize different images of the energy that surrounds our physical surroundings but never interconnect these into a meaningful web of understanding. Consider the following examples:

We and many living things depend on different forms of energy to sustain our physical bodies. Animals and humans depend on eating the food created by energy to stay alive or they will die of starvation. Plants and trees depend on water and on the sun's energy to survive.

We depend on sound wave energy produced by electrified technology to appreciate music. Humans use the energy in their vocal chords to produce sound in communicating language and songs. Humans use their physical energy to achieve great athletic feats. They also use their strength in combat and in defending their family and property. Humans have historically sought to use different energies to develop machines and technology to improve their ways of life and travelling. They continue to research how the human mind has in the past and how it can perform incredible feats. Humans have incredible creative mental energy that explains the remarkable artistic and scientific talents and masterpieces of Michelangelo and Leonardo da Vinci. There are powerful telepathic mental abilities that allow humans to communicate with each other from great distances. Humans' behavior is a paradox. They can demonstrate great human energy in acting in the sacrifice and love for each other. They are also capable of demonstrating destructive behavior caused by their anger and hatred. In the last thousand years, it is estimated there have been continuous wars in different parts of the world and approximately only 400 years of peace.

It seems that humans fail to realize that life is precious and that they possess acts of love that can elevate the human condition. Furthermore, they seem unable to connect all the other relevant dots related to the incredible physical energy environment surrounding their planet. Now with the latest attempts to explore our galaxy, we have new information and data that confirms that there are powerful forces of energy that allow the planets to maintain their orbit and prevent any abnormal movements from occurring. The earth is surrounded by a powerful gravity that acts as a shield against incoming meteors that could impact and destroy areas of our planet.

We process new information every day with fixed perceptions. We're often unaware of other viewpoints or perspectives that can expand our understanding and can impact our behavior and possibly change our style of thinking. Consider the perceptual skills and thinking that Leonardo da Vinci demonstrated. According to Bryan W. Mattimore in his article "Strategies of Genius" da Vinci trained himself to use random stimuli as provocations for creative thinking. For example, he would stare at walls spoiled with various stains or with a mixture of different kinds of stones until the mind started to see in the shaped patterns a resemblance to mountains, rivers, rocks, trees, plains, wide valleys, etc. I had a similar perceptual experience when I discovered that I was able to extract the different shapes and forms by staring at and extracting different design patterns in our shag rug.

Leonardo da Vinci also used mental associations of random events to provoke unconscious creative connections. There was one occasion

internalize. For example, the many television ads that are repeated continuously so we internalize the message never realizing that this television median is washing our brains repeatedly.

Then there are the multitude of television programs that portray situations where actors portray murder and violent behavior many times in thirty-minute sitcom or in sixty-minute movies. In this powerful cinematic environment, a youngster who is 16 years old will have visually experienced sixteen thousand murders. This powerful television median conditions their minds to accept violence as a natural occurrence in life. Consequently, they become insensitive to violent behavior. They in some cases resort to using violence to settle disagreements or to use guns to instill fear in others during robbery attempts. We continue to absorb this abnormal behavior never realizing that these young minds have become polluted. We are shocked at the number of killings of school children and teenagers by disturbed adolescents like Adam Lanza who become obsessed with acts of violence.

We are faced with a sharp increase in violent attacks by innocent people as they travel to work or in their own homes. These are serious criminal acts that are tolerated by radical district attorneys who allow these criminals to walk free and commit additional violent crimes. There must be a societal backlash to change this deterioration of a once civilized society. It is obvious that acts of violence need to be conceptualized as a mental disease that can be identified at times before it occurs. Our current news/social media and the multiple movie entities continue to project these violent depictions as a new kind of reality.

Our understanding of new behavior is related to a distorted view of how these media supposedly exist. Parents have sought to defend their children from being indoctrinated by the continuous media bombardment. There is little programming that celebrates the human ability to show sensitivity to acts of love, charity and kindness. Furthermore, we fail to correlate or associate multiple images of what a civilized society can evolve into, a meaningful web of understanding. The problem may be that our current understanding of reality is based on looking at and perceiving events through a peephole that fails to show the big picture of what is significant and relevant. When our positive Christian beliefs and opinions do not agree with the reported secular viewpoints, these become attacked and criticized as being radical. Furthermore, when these civilized points of view do not agree with different opinions, we create an adversarial communication environment. But exhortation and arguments never open minds to consider other different points of view that may offer the opportunity to develop a degree of agreement and consensus.

Consider the observation made by researcher and author Marshall McLuhan that 'the median is the message'. It may be difficult to understand the significance of this provocative opinion. Yet if we begin to appreciate its meaning and application to our peephole perception of current reality. It is obvious that this psychological stress has had an impact on the human condition. A Map of Consciousness has been recognized because it can investigate epochs of history. It can calibrate the critical levels of conscious behavior between 200 and 700 levels. Mahatma Gandi was able to force the British out of India because of his great level of human consciousness of 700 whereas the British resorted to the use of force that calibrated at a lower level of 175. Throughout history, society has treated social problems by passing laws, market manipulation, prohibitions, and even warfare, hoping that this use of force would resolve the problems. The problems persisted and recurred despite these approaches. Now there is evidence that a healing of the mind and emotions can change perception, thinking and behavior.

The focus on contemplating this Map of Consciousness will allow for developing a sense of empathy leading to a higher level of consciousness with an unconditional kindness to all life including one's own with an attitude of compassion. Without this compassion, little is ever accomplished in human endeavors. Humans with a passion for violence can fundamentally be healed and change their perceptions toward other people.

The research and millions of calibrations of David R. Hawkins have accurately recognized sets of attitudes and emotions localized by specific attractor energy fields that are understood.

Considering the problem of information anxiety that most people face, it may be possible to seek an alternative way of challenging the reality we seem obliged to accept because we fail to change our perceptual processing platform to discover new insights and ideas which could revolutionize our thinking and our perceptual behavior.

In an attempt to introduce a revolutionary way to understand how our mental energy can influence how we think and behave, I would like to share the research of Dr. David Hawkins that is presented in his book 'Power Versus Force'. He has created a Map of Consciousness where he calibrates levels that correlate with specific mental processes of consciousness-emotions, perceptions, or attitudes, worldviews, and spiritual beliefs. The chart shows different levels of energy fields that correlate with positive and negative human behavior.

Throughout history, men have implemented great spiritual disciples to help humans ascend through different levels of consciousness. Success depended on the teacher and his inspiration and instruction. Dr. Hawkins is relevant in this our search for enlightenment because it presents different levels of mental energy flow associated with our particular thoughts, feelings and associations. These are listed as follows:

Energy Level 20 – Shame
Energy Level 30 – Guilt
Energy Level 50 – Apathy
Energy Level 75 – Grief
Energy Level 100 – Fear
Energy Level 125 – Desire
Energy Level 150 – Anger
Energy Level 175 – Pride
Energy Level 310 – Willingness

Energy Level 350 – Acceptance
Energy Level 400 – Reason
Energy Level 500 – Love
Energy Level 540 – Joy
Energy Level 600 – Peace
Energy Level 700 - Enlightenment

This classification came about when Dr. John Diamond developed a new discipline that became behavioral kinesiology which helped to identify specific muscles that strengthen or weaken in the presence of negative and positive intellectual and emotional stimuli. This discovery was further developed using H. O. Kendall's "Muscle Testing and Function". The calibrated scale developed by Dr. Hawkins identifies powerful attractor fields within the human sphere of consciousness which are important in organizing mental energies from multiple patterns of human behavior. This stratification of attractor fields corresponds to different levels of human consciousness. This development provides a new paradigm for reconceptualizing our understanding of human behavior. This method of analysis has provided greater understanding as a research tool with potential use in several human activities in art, politics, history, medicine, sociology as well as in criminology, self-improvement and addictionology. This method allows for new understanding of human behavior that can be viewed and conceptualized to attain a certain verifiable truth. Kinesiology ascertains a connection between the mind and the body revealing that the mind thinks with the body. It is important to note that human behavior can fluctuate from one level to another so that a person's overall level of consciousness is the sum total of different levels in the following classifications.

Energy Level 20: SHAME

The Shame based personality is withdrawn and even shy and introverted. Shame helps to evolve into a certain vulnerability leading to negative emotions such as anger and false pride.

Energy Level 30: GUILT

The effect of guilt is that it can be used to punish and manipulate others leading to self-incrimination, masochism, and even remorse. A feeling of guilt can be a life-long condition. It can lead to rage and provoke an individual to commit murder.

Energy Level 50: APATHY

This level behavior manifests itself into a state of helplessness. This can produce despair, poverty, and even hopelessness. This is manifested in society where people have become subjected to chronic disease, old age, and being out casted from society.

Energy Level 75: GRIEF

Individuals within this level develop a sense of continuous mourning, bereavement, and remorse from events of the past. Such emotional losses can lead to serious depression and even death.

Energy Level 100: FEAR

This is the favorite tool used by totalitarian regimes to control people's thinking and behavior. Continued trepidation prevents human progress and growth. Continuous social media and advertising messages play to fear to increase market share.

Energy Level 125: DESIRE

The desire for prestige, money and power has driven many to develop insatiable desires for more wealth. Multimillionaires seem to be obsessed with acquiring more and more money.

Energy Level 150: ANGER

At this level of consciousness, people move from grief and apathy and are led to overcome social injustices, inequality, and victimization. In history, many great changes have been attained with social fury producing major movements that ushered in change.

Energy Level 175: PRIDE

Many wars were fought in the past when a sense of pride and nationalization could be encouraged by the slaughter of thousands of soldiers. Pride can lead a leader to a sense of arrogance and oppression.

Energy Level 200: COURAGE

At this level, individuals are willing to try new things and deal with the challenges and sudden changes in society. At this level, there is a willingness to learn through education and opportunities for growth.

Energy Level 250: NEUTRALITY

At this level, people want to be flexible and non-judgmental. They have a sense of well-being and demonstrate a capability to get along with others.

Energy Level 310: WILLINGNESS

At this level, individuals are willing to be helpful to others and to contribute to society. The individual has overcome the inner resistances to life and is committed to a positive participation in society.

Energy Level 350: ACCEPTANCE

At this level, there is a major transformation that an individual is the creator and the source of experience of one's life.

Energy Level 400: REASON

With the use of reason, one is capable of handling large, complex amounts of data as well as being able to make rapid and correct decisions with an understanding of the operating intricate relationships.

Energy Level 500: LOVE

Loving is a state of being. It is nurturing and a supportive way of looking at the world. It isn't intellectual but emanates from the heart. It has the capacity to lift others and realize great accomplishments.

Energy Level 540: JOY

As love becomes more unconditional, one experiences and develops a sense of inner joy. Saints and other advanced spiritual individuals and healers attain this state of being.

Energy Level 600: PEACE

In this energy field, one experiences a transcendence, self-realization and even "God" consciousness.

Energy Level 700-1000: ENLIGHTENMENT

At this level of consciousness and powerful inspiration, these individuals place powerful energy attractor fields that influence all mankind.

CHAPTER SIX

Third Eye's Ability to Alter Perception

WE OFTEN IGNORE THE ROLE that perception plays in learning. In fact, I believe that it is an area of research that continues to baffle educators, researchers, and historians. Yet this has been studied and explained by one of the great thinkers of the Renaissance, Leonardo da Vinci. He was convinced that all knowledge originates in perception. He stated devi "Sapere a Vedere', meaning that if you change the way you look at things, the things you look at change. Another great thinker, Albert Einstein, was able to advance his research by not looking at things as they are but by altering his perception to observe an imagined universe. He believed that imagination was more important than knowledge.

While we are great scientists, it is possible to train our minds to alter our perception in order to generate new insights, new ideas, and new learning. I believe that we need to believe, that we have a sixth sense that can accomplish this. I also believe that understanding the power of a Third Eye and training the mind to use this sixth sense can transform our ability to observe and see things with a fresh outlook in a way that is analogous to how we as children would perceive.

Humans behave according to how they think and feel. The information they receive from outside mass media is intentionally orchestrated to impact the way they perceive their localized reality. Most humans tend not to challenge this information bombardment from social/mass media because they lack an effective set of processing tools. We seem to have been socialized to become passive information processors during their many years of schooling. We have memorized a lot of information which we were obliged to regurgitate in school tests. Those of us that question this kind of compliance and refuse to submit are scrutinized and forced out of the system. We have lost the ability to think critically.

There is an alternative possibility that involves developing an innate visual ability that transforms the mind to accumulate visual understandings as opposed to word images that limit our brain functions. This ability has been verified in recent neurological research.

This brain mechanism involves recognizing sets of visual information patterns that decide how we understand and how we attain meaning. In order to develop this higher-level processing, an individual must learn and practice a set of processing skills that generate new insights, additional ways of perceiving a situation, a decision, and a problem. A solution or a new explanation cannot emerge unless we seek to challenge our established perception and thinking.

An ability to think outside the box. This ability helps us to overcome an attitude that is confining. It limits our potential and prevents us from jumping out of our existing paradigms. We need to understand our mind's potential. We have billions of brain neurons in our physical brain. But this power like 400 horsepower of a car is useless unless the driver is skilled in using it to realize the goal, the achievement, the completion of the task, etc. Furthermore, we need to realize that the organizing and reorganizing of information on a conceptual level also produces new entry points with which to move into an information universe filled with creative ideas and insights. The effort must be made to imagine such an "information universe" by stimulating your mind's visual perception, and by deliberately activating higher level mental functioning. When we observe a phenomenon which is of interest, we have the mental ability to understand it better by seeking to recognize new patterns of recognition not previously obvious. We can use our "mind's eyes", our skill of Mindsight, to expand our understanding and knowledge.

In the Harvard Business Review of November 2007, there is an interesting article on "Cognitive Fitness" that was cited earlier. One of the areas which are identified as being very important for executives to develop is that of patterns of recognition. The authors Roderick Gilkey and Clint Kilts indicate:

"Recent neuroimaging investigations have identified one of the engines that serve the left hemisphere performance: constellations of neurons that neuroscientists such as Elkhonan Goldberg call attractors, which mediate critical functions of the brain. They are organized to orchestrate thought and action with great efficiency and effectiveness. Together they form the basis of what the Nobel Laureate Herbert Simon referred to as pattern of recognition, which is considered to be the most powerful cognitive tool we have at our disposal."

"In most cases, schooling does not develop curiosity, delight for ambiguity, and question asking skills. Rather the thinking skill that's rewarded is figuring out the right choice that is the answer held by the person in authority, the teacher." ~ The Universe Within — Page 65~

This important processing ability has been instrumental in producing significant historical outcomes starting with the age of the Renaissance, the Enlightenment, the Declaration of Independence, the American Constitution, and other documents. These social/political changes could not have occurred if these great minds did not challenge the established thinking of the times. Furthermore, these individuals had to alter their perceptions in order to challenge current thinking. They had to stimulate their minds to create innovative changes. Their intentional curiosity led them to view another reality, a new kind of democracy based on revolutionary ideas that redefined the function of government.

This new reality involved recognizing their Creator's intelligent design of the natural world defines how we live and from which we extract the necessary nutrition and materials to survive. Now we realize that these resources are not limitless. We are aware that there is an absence of fresh water, gas/oil, minerals. Humans have been on earth less than 0.01% of the planet's existence! The Earth has been around for about one third as long as the universe itself. Earth's story began at the outset of the Hadean eon, about 4.6 billion years ago. It took 600 million years just for the earth to form crust, another 300 million years for life to really get going, thanks to the evolutionary burst known as the Cambrian explosion. Several mass extinction events and some 465 million years later, mammals finally took center stage. With the first homo sapiens appearing around 300,000 years ago, humans have only been on planet Earth for 0.0067% of its existence.

In those 300,000 years, humans were very busy. They harnessed fire and lived a nomadic existence until around the Fourth millennium BC. Since then, humans have been on a meteoric trajectory, going from hunter-gather to spacefarer in less than 6,000 years. Carl Sagan famously displayed the universe's history on a 365-day calendar, with the big bang on January 1 and our current moment starting at 12:01 am, the next year. On that timeline, it's only 10:30 pm on December 31 that humans first appear, and all of the recorded history is squeezed into just a few seconds but what an adventurous few seconds it's been.

CHAPTER SEVEN

Developing Visualized Learning

THE BOOK'S FOCUS IS ON expanding our field of perception from which higher level cognitive function begins. This developmental area is critical for expanding student skill and ability related to the learning process which remains localized in lower levels in recall/comprehension. Benjamin Bloom in organizing his well-known "Taxonomy of Intellectual Skills and Abilities" outlines a composite of seven different abilities starting with basic recall to a higher level of competency at evaluation. As a learner moves to the higher levels, there develops an increased accumulation of information which provides a greater panoramic understanding. But achieving higher level skills and abilities in taxonomy requires continued reorganization of previously learned information in order to raise students' understanding of the topic. Dr. Bloom believes that the competency level of organized instruction remains at the lower recall/comprehension levels. I contend that the reason for this lower-level capability results from an over concentration on content consumption. Not enough attention is devoted to elevating the learner's processing skill with creative abilities to create 'personal knowledge'. Instead, the learner is obliged to memorize a great deal of book information that most times is not relevant and meaningful. A consequence of this rote learning is that students are obliged to learn the tests. The ability to perceive and think creatively as the great minds did is nowhere to be found. Learners have few if any historical creative geniuses to emulate in their education.

These 'Growth Mindsets' cannot be achieved without implementing an instructional program that prioritizes 'process development' over content regurgitation. This new approach would change students' perception of their mental abilities. They would be able to operate at a higher level of learning. As their understanding increases, new associations and connections are made that were not previously obvious. As the student becomes aware of higher-level processing skills and his ability to generate information, he realized the incredible mental energy potential to raise the level of understanding of topics studied. Furthermore, this kind of processing produces an ability to articulate verbally what was learned because it is now relevant and meaningful. Then students realize that they can organize a new web of understanding without total dependence on the teacher and rote memorization. Consequently, a new 'Mindset' emerges where students have a totally different view of what experiential learning can be. Now they are able to generate their own personal perspective from the information presented. What follows is a new set of objectives to raise the quality of the instructional model of education. Some of these include:

- Focus on a higher level of information processing such as synthesis, creativity, and evaluation.
- Focus on developing the ability and skill to recognize new patterns not previously obvious. This understanding leads to greater understanding and meaning. It is obvious that many of the great minds had an incredible curiosity to learn as much as possible to recognize new information patterns which opened the doors to new discoveries and inventions.
- Focus on enhancing clarity, relevancy, and structure as design priorities in the organization of the learning process.

Therefore, it is important that we understand how genius minds "think". Psychologists have examined the notebooks, conversations and correspondence of the world's greatest thinkers. They have discovered some of the specific thinking styles that characterize their thinking.

1. Geniuses look at problems in many different ways.
2. Geniuses go beyond words and numbers. Renaissance scholars revolutionized science by going beyond conventional mathematical and verbal approaches by incorporating drawings, graphics, and diagrams in their work. Albert Einstein insisted on the use of diagrams. He believed that numbers and words as they are spoken and written did not play a significant role in his thinking process.
3. Geniuses create novel combinations similar to the active curiosity of a child with a bucket of building blocks who tries to organize different structures. The genius mind is constantly combining and recombining ideas, maps and thoughts into new possible formulations in their conscious and unconscious mind.
4. The genius thinkers find relationships between dissimilar things. They possess the ability to create juxtaposition between dissimilar subjects. This interest in connecting the unconnected enables this thinker to see things that others do not.

"Thinking visually gives the genius the flexibility to display information in different ways as shown in the diagrams of da Vinci and Galileo".

CHAPTER EIGHT

Sixth Sense as a Revolutionary Way for Mental Processing

THE FOLLOWING CREATIVE METHODS LISTED below are significant since they stimulate the processing associated with developing a sixth sense. The first method is:

1. Lateral thinking developed by Dr. Edward de Bono to develop creative thinking.
2. Metaphoric thinking.
3. Brainstorming was developed by Alex Osborne for use in the advertising industry.
4. Challenging conventional wisdom.
5. Extracting new ideas from what is interpreted.
6. Design pattern thinking.

Lateral thinking is defined as "seeking ways to solve problems by apparently illogical items." In science, many major discoveries have come about through chance observation, accident, or mistake that led to non-obvious ways of perceiving things. Dr. Edward de Bono, who coined the term lateral thinking, teaches techniques that jar normal thought patterns in problem solving and shift them to new starting points. These techniques (which can be found in his 1992 book Serious Creativity, Harper Collins) led to provocations and many alternative approaches to many problems.

Metaphoric thinking is a mental process where inherent comparisons are made between entities that are considered different classifications or categories. This ability to make connections or associations brings about a new mental construct. This mental-processing ability to synthesize or create a new understanding demonstrates high cognitive operacy.

Brainstorming involves a group of people interacting to discuss a problem in order to attempt a solution. Participants are free to say whatever comes to their minds. All thoughts are entertained in the hope that this will give rise to many new ideas, which could not be generated without this group interaction.

Challenging conventional wisdom involves questioning the current thinking about the topic. Many successful innovations came about when individuals sought to go against the existing notions about the quality of coffee, ice cream, and fruits/vegetables and develop higher quality products.

Extracting new ideas from what is interpreted in the news, in new trends, or from a series of personal or group experiences will depend largely on one's ability to see certain patterns or recognizable aspects that were not previously observable in a situation or experience.

For example, if we were to analyze the intent of the mass media to communicate new reports, we can recognize their slant or spin on the news "reportage." If you look for patterns in their news stories, you will see them as an attempt to hold your thinking about a topic (i.e., Marshall McLuhan, Understanding Media: The Extensions of Man, 1964: "The Medium is the Message).

Design pattern thinking focuses on developing an understanding of how perception impacts our thinking and how focusing on remarkable design patterns like those in nature or in visual graphics can stimulate this right side of the brain. The goal is to develop a new information-operating technique that will generate new insights and concepts that will result in greater relevancy and meaning. As we become more aware of this phenomenon, we come to realize that we can also create our own graphic design patterns to bolster and improve our important human resource, the ability to think and make sense of the world in which we live and learn.

Considering all these techniques, I believe that 'deliberate focused thinking" is a very powerful technique. Dr. de Bono makes the differentiation between creativity and lateral thinking. The former describes a result while the latter is the process to attain the result. The de Bono technique can be learned and applied. It has produced remarkable results. Some of these include the transformation of the Olympic Games from a spectator to a televised event, allowing Los Angeles to make a profit of over two hundred million. Prudential Insurance Company created "living benefits" for terminally ill patients with needed financial support to pay for their care. DuPont developed a new fiber, Kevlar, because of applying lateral thinking techniques in their research for new products. These are only a few of the advances made. What follows is an excerpt from Dr. de Bono's book The Use of Lateral Thinking, pages 13-14:

The Nature of Lateral Thinking

In the Use of Lateral Thinking, the nature of lateral thinking is shown by contrasting it with traditional vertical thinking and by giving various examples of its use. Further examples are given below:

1. An ambulance hurrying along a narrow country lane comes up behind a flock of sheep, which completely fills the lane.

    There is no way of driving the sheep off the road. How does the ambulance pass the sheep?

2. The lane beside my cottage is a blind alley, so that new visitors who drive down the lane always request my assistance when it comes to getting out, since there is not enough space to turn a car around and there are no streetlights. How else could they manage?

3. The designers of a skyscraper had not been told that it was to be used as an office block, so there were too few lifts for the number of people who wanted to use them. As a result, the staff became dissatisfied and started to leave. What could be done?

These problems are trivial in themselves. They are used as illustrations because they require no special background information, and the solution is obvious once it has been found. They are used to illustrate the process of the lateral move away from the obvious approach to a new one.

Answers:

1. In the ambulance problem, the straightforward approach is to try and get the ambulance past the sheep, for instance, by stringing out the sheep along the side of the road so that the ambulance can get passed. At worst, the ambulance could drive forward slowly enough for the sheep to get out of its way. The lateral move is to stop trying to get the ambulance past the sheep and instead try to get the sheep past the ambulance. So, it is the ambulance that stops and then the flock is turned around and the sheep filter back past the stationary ambulance.

2. Only one in ten drivers thinks of using their direction indicators to illuminate the road behind them with intermittent flashes. This is because you have to move laterally from considering them only as indicators to alternative directions. The architects and engineers, when consulted, decided that there were two possible approaches: to put in more lifts or increase the use of

existing lifts (by speeding them up, staggering working hours, etc.). Someone else, however, made a lateral move and came up with a solution that was very much easier and cheaper. Instead of considering the lifts, he moved sideways to consider the impatience of the staff. This was so effectively reduced by placing mirrors around the entrances to the lifts, with the result that there were no further complaints. The three problems discussed are almost too simple to solve. But once you have made the lateral move for yourself (or read the answer), it all seems obvious. Furthermore, once you have seen the answer, it all seems very logical. It is a fundamental characteristic of lateral thinking that the solutions it produces always seem obvious and logical in hindsight even though they may have been anything but obvious in foresight (for example, only one in ten drivers used their indicators).

The reason for this is that the human mind works as a patterning system (as will be explained later), and in a patterning system, the route from A to B is not the same as the route from B to A. It is precisely this difficulty in reaching a solution that should have been obvious that makes lateral thinking an innovative technique.

In his book The Use of Lateral Thinking, Dr. Edward de Bono makes some very interesting observations of people who made some interesting discoveries and inventions. Charles Darwin's discovery is the first cited. Charles Darwin's twenty years devoted to developing his theory of evolution was eclipsed by a research paper written by Alfred Russel Wallace, which presented a clear exposition of the theory of evolution by survival of the fittest. Wallace worked out a theory of evolution by survival of the fittest. Wallace worked out the theory in one week during a state of delirium in the East Indies when suddenly he may have had a flash of insight that allowed him to look at how species survive in a totally new way.

Alexander Fleming worked with Sir Almroth Wright, a well-known bacteriologist who was developing the theory and practice for inoculation against infections. This association was instrumental in his search for all antibiotics against casualty infections, which were hard to cure. In the many observations he made during the First World War, he cultured a bacteria and he discovered lysozyme a natural antibiotic. From this discovery, he went on to discover another antibiotic: penicillin, which was perfected in the Second World War as a highly effective antibiotic.

Marconi developed equipment that could send wireless messages over long distances. When he made an attempt at transmitting a signal across the Atlantic Ocean, experts in the field believed it would not succeed because these wireless waves, like light, traveled in straight lines and would stream off into space because of the curvature of the earth. But Marconi was convinced that somehow it would work. And it did due to the fact that when the wireless signal hit the upper electrically charged layer of the upper atmosphere (ionosphere), they bounced back, and this allowed the completion of the communication. The idea of a wireless transatlantic communication had been suggested by Balfour Stewart many years before Marconi's attempt, but the idea was ahead of its time.

Albert Einstein, according to Dr. de Bono, did no experiments, gathered no new information before he created the theory of relativity. Since he never performed any experiments, he contributed little except a novel way of looking at scientific information that was available from the work of other scientists (e.g., the Michelson-Morley experiments of 1881-1887, which led to the development of the Lorentz-Einstein transformation equations and ultimately to the solution to the postulates of the special theory of relativity). Einstein was not content with the Newtonian theoretical structure. He ultimately created an improved model that led to a better understanding of the conservation of mass and energy in relativistic physics and how light waves are affected by gravitational fields (the dense star Sirius). Einstein's theories made a minimal contribution at first, but his novel ways of evaluating existing information, combined with the contributions of Heisenberg, led to our current understanding of atomic energy.

Louis Pasteur investigated many diseases, including chicken cholera and rabies. He was very observant in his investigations. In one instance, one of his assistants was careless with a culture of chicken cholera germs, and he noticed the culture lost its power to cause an outbreak of the disease. The weakened culture was able to protect chickens against infection. This discovery led to the idea of protection against disease by inoculation.

There are some interesting lessons to be learned from all these examples. The first is that we can develop new ideas by evaluating accepted models. The second lesson to be learned, according to de Bono, is the "new ideas" come about only sporadically, even when the technology that makes them possible has been available for a long time. The third is that the ability to generate new ideas is manifested in some people but not in others. The fourth point is that some great ideas and scientific discoveries occur when individuals ignore the focus on currently accepted paradigms and look for new interpretations (i.e., what- ifs). Fifth, we should allow the mind to absorb information from many sources, as in the case of divergent thinking, even if the information seems unimportant and irrelevant. Reluctance to accept new ideas is analogous to refusing to invest in new ideas that can improve how we do things. A sixth point is that many great ideas come after the new information gathered by observation or experimentation results in a breakdown of currently accepted rules/paradigms.

We can't solve problems by using the same kind of thinking we used to create them.

~Albert Einstein~

James J. Mapes, in his book Quantum Leap Thinking, has collected ideas, concepts, and skills in the hope that by combining them like chemicals, there will be a powerful reaction/explosion that will catapult the thinker to a higher level of awareness of what is possible when there is a deliberate intention to do so. He explains: This potential reality is available to all of us if we master the skills necessary to "see" all the options available and then make the most empowering "choice." The idea of making a "Quantum Leap" requires developing and maintaining "survival skills," involving creative thinking.

Continuous thinking and managing change are defined as creative thinking, the ability to see something not seen before, bringing something new out of the arrangement of the old. In his explanation of what creative thinking involves, James Mapes makes the claim that we have a creative nature that includes intuition, ideas, dreams, fantasy and invention. "Without the creative side of your brain, intelligence is rather a useless tool.

Considering all these, I believe that "recognizing patterns" is the most interesting because we should recognize that almost everything around us is organized into patterns - our language communication, our musical compositions, our dwellings, our clothing, our sense of time - and our bodies of knowledge are organized around design patterns. If we consider scientific discoveries, scientific analyses of historical events and outstanding works of art, we realize they are the result of human efforts to recognize new design patterns that were not previously apparent. The same realization occurs when listening to a humorous explanation, we suddenly recognize a new unexpected pattern between the initial statement and the unexpected punch line. The personal response is laughter.

Dr. Edward de Bono offers an interesting analysis:

A great many new ideas come about when new information gathered by observation of experiment forces a reappraisal of the old ideas. New information is probably the surest road to new ideas, but it is still unreliable, mostly if the new information is explained by the old theory and fashioned to support the theory,

Once a new idea springs into existence, it cannot be unthought. There is a sense of immortality in a new idea. There is a capacity for generating new ideas that is better developed in some people than in others. This capacity does not seem to be related to sheer intelligence but more to a particular habit of mind, a particular way of thinking.

Dr. de Bono describes this creative thinking to be a special part of lateral thinking. Creative thinking, he explains, "often requires a talent for expression, whereas lateral thinking is open to everyone who is interested in new ideas." He makes it clear that lateral thinking is an attitude, a habit of mind.

I personally believe that one of the first steps in making creative breakthroughs involves challenging assumptions. The problem is that there are only a few of us who are willing to make the effort. We don't have the time, we do not want to rock the boat, we like to leave well enough alone. There are others who disagree with this perception. Some conventional wisdom says that some people are simply born with certain gifts while others are not; that talent and high intelligence are somewhat scarce like gems scattered throughout the human gene pool. The best we can do is to locate and polish these gems and accept the limitations built into the rest of us.

While I agree that some are born with "genius potential," I also believe that this incredible ability was nurtured and developed due to certain attitudes and behaviors that helped them to become outstanding in their fields. David Shenk explains the greatness of a baseball player, Ted Williams.

Ted Williams was said to have laser-like eyesight, which enabled him to read the spin of the ball as it left the pitcher's fingers and to gauge exactly where it would pass over the plate. Williams attributed this ability to nothing but practice, practice, etc. "The reason I saw things was that I was so intense. It was discipline, not super eye."

David Shenk provides an interesting explanation about human potential:

Each human child is his/her own unique genetic entity conceived in his/her own distinctive environment, immediately spinning out his/her own unique interactions and behaviors. Who among these children born today will become great pianists, novelists, botanists, or marathoners? Who will live a life of utter mediocrity? Who will struggle to get by? We do not know.

I do believe that many genius minds have this insatiable curiosity to find an explanation, a solution, an innovation. They live and sleep this quest. This kind of extreme mental operacy creates a stream of continuous flow of new insights and information that expands their perception and understanding. With this new web of meaning, they are capable of thinking at a high level of cognitive operacy.

In preparing this manuscript, I realized the need to change the focus of many chapters because I believed that my objective in researching and writing was to instill a curiosity and desire to rekindle that "childlike perception" we once had of the world around us. As mentioned previously, I believe the natural world that surrounds us is too often taken for granted. We see no pattern and connection in the visual designs of trees, plants, butterflies/insects, and other living creatures that surround us. Now some of us have a different perception because we know that they and we are interconnected in a designed ecosystem that must be maintained if all living things in the system are to survive. If we recognize its remarkable structure, order, and interconnections, we can use these qualities to focus on in our creative pursuits. Yet artists and other creative individuals have expressed this connectedness, this idea of one with nature. They would spend hours observing living plants and animals to develop an in-depth understanding. Claude Monet is reputed to have painted fifteen different pictures of the identical haystack at different times of the day.

CHAPTER NINE
FOCUS ON VISUALIZED LEARNING

WE LIVE AND THINK IN a literal word culture which becomes more established as we become socialized and educated in our American culture. This creates a unique mindset that greatly impacts our perception of what the meaning is of such ideas as happiness, intelligence, love, success, and even meaning for our existence. But we often fail to realize that our minds are not only processing word meanings but also Powerful Visual Images that we tend to avoid recognizing and exploring. In many ways, these visual images have already impacted human evolution beginning with the historic French cave drawings describing animal images but also the Egyptian many animal/humanoid images and symbols. Early communities of American Indians also inscribed animal pictorials on stone surfaces but also inserted animal images in creatively designed headdresses. Alaskan Indians carve tall wooden statues to honor their historical past.

Today we still promote animal images by producing children's documentaries and cartoons with familiar Disney characters that we have learned to love. It seems that even parents are watching these animal portrayals that tend not to depict the violence and destruction of life. Maybe for this reason, these films seem to be more relevant because they portray another image of imagined peaceful creatures. It seems that we are beginning to transition from the established word socialization and accumulation which at times creates an overload limiting our ability to achieve meaning.

Saul Wurman describes a current American culture filled with "Information Anxiety" unable to attain understanding. Many individuals fail to realize that we are living in a new social technological environment where new ideas are becoming a currency of the future. Many people do not realize that we are working and living in a new creative paradigm that requires new ideas, new procedures and ways of thinking. One of these is that we are slowly transitioning from an established printed word culture to a creative visual environment where society is attracted to action packed visual images that characterize current TV ads organized to manipulate the minds of the television viewers. This attraction is not new since historically humans have used visual depictions to express their beliefs and their thinking. In this new millennium, we realize that visual images and symbols are worth more than a thousand words. In scientific conferences scientists will use graphic images to better communicate their ideas and their particular points of view.

Peter Drucker had previously prophesized this information revolution would occur. But it would not involve technological advances. In his publication, Information and Entrepreneurship, he explains that this forthcoming information transformation will involve the creation of new ideas. Joel Barker describes the shift to a new paradigm brought on by visionary thinkers who through history turned their dreams into powerful visions of how humans can interact in their pursuit of creative expression and innovation. This concept was further discussed by Thomas Kuhn in his publication, "The Structure of Scientific Revolution" where he explains why society has not always been able to lead to scientific breakthroughs but that lateral thinkers like Galileo and Columbus challenged established knowledge with new concepts and new ways of visualizing the physical world.

Ideas and concepts have an energy in and of themselves. They gather their power from the minds that developed them. Some of the great changes in world history came about as a result of unique concepts which influenced and changed people's thinking. Jesus, Gandhi, Lincoln, Jefferson, Martin Luther King and others promoted a new perception and plan for human behavior. Their ideas and innovative concepts had an almost gravitational attraction in human society. Many times, novel ideas start as a kind of provocation which shakes current thinking and behavior. This provocation opens the minds to consider a new way of thinking about existing established notions. This experience eventually changes existing human perception and behavior once the new insight is adopted. At times innovative ideas seem ridiculous at first sight. Yet with time, they become acceptable when the percentage of believers passes critical mass 18 stage.

There is always the possibility that we will enter a new paradigm where our perception will focus on the physical intelligent design that surrounds us. We are told that everything we know is interconnected. Yet, we remain disconnected. Consequently, we do not develop a higher mental cognitive understanding. We do not enhance our web of understanding with new insights and meaning. We seem to be listening to the same psychological tune, hoping that technology will create a new kind of music that elevates the human mind. The reality is the opposite is happening. Our perceptual skills and creative thinking is in the necessary cognitive development. Our children are being deprived of the necessary cognitive development necessary to survive in the new millennium with all its demanding decisions and social indoctrination that impacts their lives in a negative way.

I believe that the solution requires a new way of looking at the physical world that surrounds us in much the same way that the great thinkers of the past like Leonardo da Vinci who believed that this is possible if we change our perception to see things differently. For example, consider the intelligent design in nature. When we pass by a forest of similar size trees, we fail to see those similar patterns of shape, size and texture. This remarkable design pattern supports the idea in nature is interconnected. Yet we fail to learn from visual design phenomena.

CHAPTER TEN

Creative Thinking of Leonardo da Vinci

IT IS IMPORTANT WE UNDERSTAND how genius minds "think". Psychologists have examined the notebooks, the conversations, and the correspondence of the world's greatest thinkers. They have discovered some of the specific thinking styles that characterize their thinking:

1. Geniuses look at problems in many different ways.

2. Geniuses go beyond words and numbers. Renaissance scholars revolutionized science by going beyond conventional mathematical and verbal approaches by incorporating drawings, graphics, and diagrams into their work. Albert Einstein insisted on the use of diagrams. He believed that numbers and words as they are spoken and written did not play a significant role in his thinking process.

3. Geniuses create novel combinations similar to the active curiosity of a child with a bucket of building blocks who tries to organize different structures. The genius mind is constantly combining and recombining ideas, maps and thoughts into new possible formulations in their conscious and unconscious mind.

4. The genius thinkers find relationships between dissimilar things. They possess the ability to create juxtaposition between dissimilar subjects. This interest in connecting the unconnected enables this thinker to see things that others do not.

"Thinking visually gives the genius the flexibility to display information in different ways as shown in the diagrams of da Vinci and Galileo".

One of the traits of a genius mind is the ability or skill to calculate proportions in a different physical dimension. Leonardo da Vinci developed this skill in order to figure out the design and function of whatever was under investigation. This awareness of spatial relationships was enhanced by his artistic depictions shown in his notebooks which were filled with continuous sketches and drawings. His creative mind quickly developed an ability to calculate distances, shapes and designs. This information was transmitted telepathically through his arms to his fingertips which effectively illustrated the ideas and designs he extracted.

"Leonardo believed that drawing is a scientific and superior demonstrative instrument far superior to the word. Drawings achieve perfection over what a writer faces in his oral discourse. This figurative discourse alternated his oral discourse resulting in fragmented thoughts alongside the thousands of unrelated notes."

As mentioned previously, Leonardo was fascinated with different designs he studied and their respective functions. He possessed an incredible visual ability that was demonstrated in the detailed notations in many of his notebooks. Where we see visual objects, his mind sees those objects in their particular linear designs. It is obvious he saw things through another visual dimension. This perspective allowed him to extract new insights, new creative possibilities that other scientists could not envision. He continued his practice of observing and documenting new details. This continuous mental processing transformed his mind resulting in genius abilities that produced innovative design and depictions in the painting the Mona Lisa, the Last Supper.

His anatomical analysis of the human body made it possible to rediscover how the bodies' mechanics correspond to emotion according to the exact muscular movements. Here as in other places, Leonardo seems to value the importance of perception and the need for balance so that every muscle varies in volume according to whether or not it is in motion.

Leonardo was continuously curious to figure out nature's inner operations. He spent considerable time observing phenomena to better understand what he was. Leonardo would observe a bird's physical flying skills from initial take-off, during flight and he watched as they corrected their approach to a landing on a tree or on different physical objects. He must have wondered how they could figure out distances of spaces in order to adjust their landing speed. He soon realized that the creatures possessed a certain form of intelligence because they rarely made mistakes in their landing approach. He probably rarely saw birds crash into each other as they flew in formations over large distances. Leonardo was able to quantum leaps in his understanding of the natural environment around him. He could exact the maximum suggestive qualities freely expressed producing extraordinary painting with a vision of perpetual action. His method is representative in hundreds of drawings. In this illustration previously mentioned portrays the head of a horse with nostrils with fiercely upturned nostrils alongside the head of a roaring lion and the face of a screaming man. All three images create a very compelling sequence of "photograms". The result is that the drawings become more expressive and more intelligible than similar literal descriptions.

The key parts of visual thinking process include the eye, the brain, the hand and capability to modify the information that is being processed through the communication loop.

One of the traits of an analytical mind is the ability or skill to calculate proportions in different physical dimensions. Leonardo da Vince developed this skill in order to figure out the design and function of whatever he was investigating. There was, I believe, a fascination with the different designs he studied and their respective function. He possessed an incredible skill to make detailed notation of what he saw. When we see physical objects like trees, his mind sees these designs in their particular geometric designs. It is obvious he saw things through another scientific dimension. This perspective allowed him to extract new insights, new creative possibilities that other scientists could not envision. He carefully recorded all his observations and continued to add new details that were not previously obvious. This continuous mental processing transformed his mental processing ability to document what previously was not understood.

The study of nature leads us to a realization of a Dive mind. The imitation of nature impacts the mind of the painter, the creative character of this divine mind. Leonardo was always fascinated by the intelligent design in nature. He studied nature as if he were a pupil who wants to discover the secrets of nature in order to compete with this divinity in inventing and painting pictures that pulsate with life even in the machines and devices he produced where inert material comes alive.

Observational Skills as the Key to Receiving New Patterns of Recognition

If we take a closer look at nature, we see that it is also full of patterns, symmetry and order. Some creatures are almost perfectly symmetrical like a sea star and other echinoderms with identical limbs. Of all the 2,000 species of sea stars living in the ocean, most have five arms. Beyond the animal world, the snowflake is perhaps one of the best-known icons of symmetry formed from water crystals when water solidifies into crystals under certain conditions.

"The cerebral cortex which accounts for 80 percent of the human brain is composed of a highly repetitive structure, allowing humans to create arbitrating complex structure of ideas". ~ David Shenk~

We seem to assume that intelligence is the result of our evolved mental operacy. We identify and label people as intelligent based on their ability to solve problems and deal with difficult challenges. Yet, some of these individuals get caught in an "intelligent trap" because they tend to use their intelligence to defend their point of view. This confines their thinking to an established mind-set where they are unable to observe other points of view, other possibilities, etc. This inability to look beyond the obvious is a perceptual problem that can be remedied by looking beyond the obvious or by viewing existing data with another set of spectacles.

"Logic is a tool invested for certain uses. It is not the way we deal with reality most of the time despite our conditioning". ~Alfred Adler~

As thinkers, we are consciously and unconsciously searching for meaning and identification. The goal of our information search is to create a web of meaning and understanding of "how things fit together". In this search, we are in the state of continuous mental activity in thinking out, in sorting out and figuring out. Imagine for a moment that we are virtually orbiting in a "universe of ideas and concepts", organizing and reorganizing information daily. Those of us who have an insatiable appetite know more and to figure out more can do so by developing higher thinking processes. Leonardo da Vinci, (How to Think Like Leonardo) believed, as stated previously, that dealing with ambiguity and uncertainty was one of the first steps to achieve clarity and to finding the truth, "knowing how to see...", looking beyond the obvious...sharpen your senses to improve your mind. There was a period of reflection on the arts in the second quarter of the 15th century. This enables da Vinci to formulate concepts, precise guidelines in matters related to painting but also to sculpture, architecture, etc.

Leonardo da Vinci was of the opinion that basic understanding involved the developing of multiple points of view and the subsequent analyses of them led to complete and true knowledge. In designing the bicycle, he considered the opinions of the individuals sponsoring the prototype for production, the consumers who would purchase it, and the municipalities where the bicycles would be used. These multiple points of view increased his understanding and awareness of the required objectives that needed to be satisfied by his bicycle. His multiple considerations raised the quality of his thinking and represented an important step in the creative design process.

Da Vinci was continuously challenging the accepted point of view which probably maintained that sketching the three images on the same page made little sense. In retrospect considering the recent discoveries of the brain's neurosciences, it is likely that Leonardo was implementing this powerful processing skill. As he developed this high-level ability, he sought to devote his curiosity to make new connections in his scientific pursuits but also in his continuous observations of all the intelligent designs within the natural world. He became fascinated by the wealth of new knowledge that could be discovered and applied using this new ability. During his lifetime, he made over six thousand entries in his notebooks which show an intelligence far advanced even during the Renaissance period. He firmly believed that this ability could be developed. He suggested that it had to do with how we perceived what we saw. He saw things with a set of "creative spectacles". If we changed the way we viewed things, the things we viewed would change.

Another excellent example is evident in the invention of the fastener by George de Mestral in the 1940s. He and his dog brushed up against a bush that had burrs that stuck to his dog and his clothing and thereby created a problem because they were difficult to remove. Upon viewing the burrs under a microscope, he discovered hundreds of small hooks on each burr that would snag on to anything touching it.

Charles Darwin advanced his theory on evolution by focusing on an image of a tree to reorganize his thoughts in documenting his research. This allowed him to gather new insights by pulling in unrelated information. Each of these graphic representations was meaningful in his search for what was not known about evolution.

David Hawkins in his publication Power vs. Force provides us with some insights as to why we wrestle with this process of knowing:

Although we ascribe our actions to reason, man in fact operates primarily out of pattern of recognition, the logical arrangement of data serves mainly to enhance a pattern of recognition system that then becomes "truth." But nothing is ever true except under the circumstances, and then only from a particular viewpoint, characteristically unstated.

CHAPTER ELEVEN
Visual Expressions and Concepts as Information Spectacles

HUMAN BEINGS IN THEIR EVOLUTION have sought to develop skills in order to survive as a species in competition with their environment and other creatures. In the early development of tools, humans have sought to use sharp edges of stones to cut game. They have organized hunts so as to ensure their successful kill. They have expressed the desire to communicate their experiences. The pictorial evidence of their hunting experience was more than an expression. This concept of the hunt demonstrates their particular visual sense of time and space, showing an advanced mental functioning of the "early man". These cave drawings allow us to understand their story but also their desire to transfer this story of the hunt. It shows an inner urge to communicate "visual concepts". This intent becomes very significant since it later leads to an elaborate communication system, which evolves into a written system and literature. With the invention of the printing press, the interest in reading and learning increases. This leads to centers of learning and universities.

"Whatever exists in the universe, in essence, in appearance, in imagination, the painter has first in his mind and then in his hand".
~Leanardo da Vinci~

We are in some ways in the same dilemma as our early cave dwellers. We seek to use concepts. We have learned to be better at what we do. While we don't draw on the walls of our homes, we seek to listen and practice the "mental depictions" that contemporary popular authors offer, as these are frames of reference for our own mental consumption. People seem very interested in improving their emotional and psychological state of mind through self-help books filled with psychological concepts. They attend seminars offered by popular "mind development" authors such as Anthony Robbins, Deepak Chopra, Stephen Covey, etc. All of this seems to show a desire for expanding their mental powers by implementing concepts in order to survive in this complex information/technological age which pressures us to be better parents, workers, professionals, mates, leaders, etc. It is a race without a finish.

"The physical entities, which seem to serve as elements of productive thought are certain signs and more or less clear images which can be voluntarily reproduced and combined. These cognitive elements are visual and some muscular type." ~Albert Einstein~

In our interactions with others, we act on a daily basis according to how we feel and think. We have a "blueprint" of values, attitudes and beliefs that condition our thinking. Within this "blueprint" are powerful concepts established in our minds derived from our education and our experience and our upbringing.

"The Brain acts as a laboratory. it's an architect, it designs models, and it puts pieces together" ~Joe Dispenza~

What are the concepts? How do they function? How can we utilize their "processing dynamics" to expand our intelligence and our own "information processors?" Concepts are abstractions drawn in many cases from our physical environment. "Whiteness" is an abstraction drawn from those things we perceive as being white...e.g. snow, a wedding dress, vanilla ice cream, paper, white ceiling, etc. We tend to view the external world with our particular set of concepts that are a summation of our knowledge and experience in our contemporary society. We have established laws, theories, concepts which form our operating paradigm. Some thinkers question the existing paradigms, trying to create awareness of the new emerging paradigms. These paradigms have implications for how we think and live. In a constantly changing world, we seek to constantly organize and reorganize information and data into new webs of meaning. Some individuals who are aware of these organizing webs also realize the importance of generating new information, extracting new concepts and of making new connections between things that were obvious and those that weren't. Some individuals use creative concepts as their "mental triggers" to create "movement" in the mind, going from less information. However, it is the mental activity of organizing and reorganizing data and information as "a mental operacy" that demonstrates our curiosity and intent to understand things better, to apply and analyze concepts, and eventually to create something that did not exist in our-conscious mind. Scientists, artists, musicians, writers, etc., spend countless hours consciously seeking those "breakthrough" insights, which lead to a discovery or great artistic expressions --a "Masterpiece".

"Almost a fifth of all classical music performed in modern times were written by just three composers: Bach, Mozart and Beethoven."   *-David K. Simonton-*

We applaud and are in awe of these great thinkers because of what they have achieved with their minds. Einstein, da Vince, Michelangelo, Edison, and Hemmingway gave us insights about the skills and the abilities that they utilized. Einstein believed his imagination was his great gift, the ability to imagine what hadn't been. This ability was used in his famous thought experiments, e.g. riding on a beam of light. DaVinci spoke of the importance of perception, how we can learn to consciously see patterns not evident before. da Vinci conceptualized drawings of machines and devices that were hundreds of years ahead of their time. Edison built machines applying creative concepts not realized previously. However, the common desire they all had was a driving force to use their creative skills and abilities. They consciously and deliberately pushed their minds to their maximum output. The effort allowed them to move to the outer limits of existing paradigms in pursuit of their "creative breakthroughs."

"Einstein suggested a certain connection "between" the physical entities which seem to serve as elements in thought and relevant logical concepts."
~R. Bernstein~ "Sparks of Genius"

There is however another aspect to consider besides their awareness and deliberateness and that is they were working with creative concepts and operating in "an unexplored information universe." The human mind can do this without difficulty once we develop this higher-level mental functioning. The trick or the goal is to become convinced that your creative mind has this ability and you have only to "drive it" accordingly. "Simple to say but difficult to do," may be the reaction of most readers. Such an attitude is confining. It limits our potential and prevents us from jumping out of our paradigms. We need to understand our mind's potential. We have possession of millions of brain neurons in our physical brain. But this power, like 400 horsepower of a car, is useless unless the driver is skilled in using it to realize the goal achievement, the completion of the task, etc. Furthermore, we need to realize that the organizing and reorganizing of information on a conceptual level also produces new entry points with which to move into an information universe filled with creative ideas and insights. The effort must be made to imagine such an "information universe", by stimulating your mind's visual perception and by deliberately activating higher level mental functioning. When we observe a phenomenon which is of interest, we have the mental ability to understand it better by seeking to recognize new patterns of recognition not previously obvious. We can use our "mind's eyes", our skill of Mindsight, to expand our understanding and knowledge.

Yet these Renaissance thinkers developed a keen interest in observing and studying the unique physical phenomena that surrounded them as opposed to solely reading from the established depictions. We seem to have forgotten the importance and relevance that the skill of observation had in the Renaissance. Many great discoveries, scientific advances, and remarkable inventions were made by recognizing the many unique design patterns existing in nature. These creative minds were continually looking to explain these intelligent designs because they believed that this mental effort stimulated their minds to develop new insights, new ideas, new images. The result was that the Renaissance produced incredible artistic innovations, new technologies, and new architectural designs. It also created a renewed interest in exploring the unknown parts of the planet. Christopher Columbus was one of these early explorers who rejected the idea that the earth was flat. He sought to travel a different route and he discovered a new continent. His perception and thinking challenged existing beliefs that the earth was flat. He was a "lateral thinker" who challenged this notion and logical thinking that was current. He sought to think out of the box and imagine another reality. His ability to imagine a different planet was the symbolic trait of many great Renaissance thinkers who challenged established mindsets.

CHAPTER TWELVE

THE CREATIVITY EXPLORATORY POWER OF THE THIRD EYE

THERE ARE SO MANY THINGS to learn and sometimes we seem unable to see what is obvious. Recent research has identified a powerful brain mechanism that decides how we attain meaningful understanding. It is composed of millions of neurons called attractors that work together to create an awareness of some insight that was not evident. It is called Pattern Recognition and was discovered by a former Nobel laureate Herbert Simon who considered this to be the most powerful cognitive processing tool. It involves the brain's ability to scan the environment to identify order and to create meaning from existing data and knowledge. This neurological chain reaction operates at the highest level of abstraction and thinking. It is a critical competency that delves into the deepest depository of stored knowledge and experience. It can become a powerful technique to improve our ability to become creative thinkers capable of articulating new ideas and concepts.

We possess a powerful Third Eye that opens our mind to new understandings of the world in which we live. This third Eye has the ability to connect the many visual images which create new insights, new understanding, and a new awareness previously unknown. Consider an obvious notion we know of but were unable to understand its relevance. We are aware of motion and movement. We see many examples but are unaware of the undiscovered associations or recognizable patterns. We activate our bodies every day to accomplish critical tasks. But within his body there is continuous intake of 2,000 gallons of air to draw oxygen to keep our internal organs operating. Then there is movement of 5 gallons of blood throughout our body to our extremities. To achieve this blood flow, it is calculated that the heart pumps 10,000 times a day. In order to keep this incredible system operating, we have to feed our bodies with nutrients in order to provide the required energy to stay alive. But all animals, including birds, mammals, plants, trees, fish, insects will suffer disease and death if they are unable to move about to find food containing needed nutrients. Birds fly thousands of miles to warmer climates and return in the spring to nest and feed their young. Enormous whales swim to new parts of the planet in search of food. African herds travel hundreds of miles in search of new pastures. The planet earth with a defined flight pattern, moves 4,800 miles around our sun every year. Our galaxy moves through an infinite universe filled with millions of other galaxies.

We are not cognizant of this complex movement, probably due to the fact that we see everything through a peephole that doesn't provide this more panoramic picture of this basic notion that defines our existence. The use of our Third Eye allows us to see things in more recognizable patterns. Consequently, our mind is then able to process more information into an innovative visual design. This effort produces new awareness and new understandings that raise our cognitive ability. However, this higher level mental 'operacy' requires us to accept that we can learn and think in visual terms. Many of the great thinkers like Galileo, Leonardo da Vinci, Copernicus, Newton, Darwin and Einstein, Menobolt observed or imagined visual phenomena. Their visual thinking produced new discoveries and monument understandings.

I often wondered why Albert Einstein believed that words were most useful in figuring out the universe. It is possible that he realized that thinking in a visual dimension would open his mind to a new virtual reality. He stated that imagination was more important than knowledge.

Einstein's research focused on the physical forces in the universe. He challenged the accumulated knowledge of his time. He sought to figure things out by organizing multiple visual thought experiments where he imagined himself falling in an elevator or flying on a stream of light or looking out the window of a Swiss trolley moving at the changing visual images. He was curious to investigate the phenomena of movement. He discovered that energy was the vital force of the universe. He believed energy was the foundation of all existence.

Today we are living and working in a new Creative Paradigm. It was promoted by scientific and technical inventions that stimulated creative design thinking. This new opportunity to create new insights and understandings. Scientific observations in Quantum physics and new research in neurosciences made this possible.

A second Renaissance ushered in a new way of thinking about our current evolution. Human beings were no longer considered self-contained independent entities but now were focal points in a united field of matter and energy. They were inseparable, interconnected with patterns of intelligence in the whole cosmos. Humans were one set of many relationships. We were a part of the universal body. Our minds were an extension of the universal mind. Our thoughts were impulses of intelligence as quantum events in a unified field.

What we learn is tied to the skill of perception learned. We are more than egos and personalities. Human consciousness is characteristic of many parts of the changing scenery. We are not the scenery but the Seer who creates and witnesses the changing scenery. We live in a participatory universe. The objective world is created by the response of the observer.

We have discovered a universe that is composed of energy fields. These operate from one underlying field where space and time exist in a cosmos that is infinite and unbounded. Yet we remain trapped in the old paradigm reality, unable to imagine that there is a totally different incredible operating universe in which to participate. This inability to think differently has to do with being socialized into a society that is unwilling to implement a virtual Third Eye that can develop new insights and understanding required to operate in a new creative paradigm. We need to realize that creative ideas are becoming the currency of the future.

CHAPTER THIRTEEN

Sixth Sense and Practical Wisdom

THE PRACTICAL WISDOM OF THE Shamans of Mexico was explained in the popular publications of Carlos Casteneda. I chose to insert their teachings because they stress the redeployment of energy as the first step in order to develop mental alertness, physical prowess and adequate muscular condition. This is important because every part of the human body is engaged in some way in turning the vibratory flow of energy into a kind of sensory input which with practice is transformed into a system of interpretation that allows human beings to become capable of perceiving the world which becomes the cornerstone of knowledge. They believed as Leonardo da Vinci did that all knowledge begins in perception.

The Shamans believed that seeing this energy flow in the universe was the essential tool needed for perceiving the different energy configurations which exist in different layers. These fields are not accessible because in our daily world experience which become part of man's natural heritage. The teaching of the Shaman is to create a human energetic configuration to allow for the development of luminous balls seeing the flow of energy in the universe so as to identify the true self in this configuration.

This conglomerate of energy fields is analogous to the classifications of energy fields presented by Dr. David Hawkins in his book 'Force vs. Power'. In the Shamans interpretation, the redeployment of energy is a critical issue in their lives as well as in the lives of human beings. This intended transformation consists of moving from one energy field to another. This potential already exists within us. Our existing energy field has displaced us from the centers of vitality in the body necessary if we are to develop a balance between mental alertness and physical prowess. In order to develop this balance between audacity and recklessness, a Sharman has to be extremely sober, cautious, skillful and in great physical condition.

Shamans believed that observing energy directly allows one to turn energy into sensory data and then begin to interpret it. They further believed that perception begins at an assemblage point which is located behind the shoulder blades, an arm's length from them. And at this point, humans have an entirely similar view of the world which develops from usage and socialization. This arbitrary position one develops an illusion that is final and irreducible. Consequently, humans have an unshakeable conviction that the world they encounter is the only one that exists. This translates into a belief that only this world exists and that its finality is undeniable. The Shamans realized that seeing the energy flows in the universe is the challenging tool that a lineage of Shamans pursued. This activity allowed them to discover that there are a staggering number of worlds out there for humans to perceive. Consequently, it is possible to discover and struggle with where one can act and die as in this world of everyday life, we find it hard to make this reality leap because as stated previously, we perceive and think through words. Consider the following visual perspectives of energy that are not obvious:

Every living species needs energy in the form of water and food as well as sunlight in order to survive. Each of these living entities secretes a form of energy which is never wasted because it is recycled to nourish other living things. Every plant and tree that is alive provides us with a form of nutritional energy that is indispensable. When any living thing dies, it releases its energy which in the case of plants and trees is recycled into new emerging living specimens. When humans cease to exist, their energy is released in the form of a spiritual energy that continues to function in another 'virtual dimension'. When we think positive thoughts, we produce a positive mental energy. Prayer is one example. Human expressions and acts of love and compassion often can impact the lives of others in a very powerful way. Negative thoughts, humiliating verbal behavior and violent actions against others produces powerful destructive outcomes.

While we operate as physical entities, we are in great need of love and affection from birth because this feeds our emotional and mental wellbeing. It also impacts our 'spiritual existence' since I believe that we are spirits living temporarily in physical bodies. So, when we show love and compassion for another person, this emotional expression frees up that spiritual energy and makes the recipient feel special, especially since it was not expected.

As we transform our verbal understanding of the word energy into a Visual Concept, we realize that it has a more comprehensive meaning. This mental transformation raises our understanding to a higher cognitive level as it did for Albert Einstein.

CHAPTER FOURTEEN

Visual Indoctrination Promotes Some Violence in A Civilized Society

I, LIKE MANY, AM TRYING to understand why there is this increase in the use of violence at this point in the evolution of the human species. One obvious explanation is that our species is regressing. One possible reason is that humans have lost one of their most important resources, their ability to utilize a critical mental processing ability to figure things out. When faced with apparent personal losses and impending tragedies, they lack an ability to develop creative thinking to confront serious situations at different stages of their lives.

Then there is another explanation. The human mind has been seriously manipulated by new technology i.e. television, computers, mobile phones, the internet that has entered their homes and their ability to develop a personal web of understanding and a search for meaning in their lives. Many humans have evolved into psycho robots who have a distorted perspective on what it means to be human in terms of an ability to love, to empathize, to forgive, to seek personal development at the different stages of their lives.

There is increased concern for the increased acts of violence against women involved in troubled relationships. We seem to have devalued the significance of human life considering the fact that we abort millions of fetuses, that we allow our children to watch thousands of murders by the time they reach the age of sixteen. We also promote video games where the aim is to destroy or eliminate the opposing attacking forces. Consider also the increased use of dangerous weapons as a method to resolve differences or opinions, mutual disagreements, and an inability to seek other possible solutions to emerging discontent in a relationship.

It is obvious that realistic solutions are necessary. For example, is there a need to educate students with a curriculum that engenders a belief that every human person is to be give respect and love as that is a fundamental belief and commandment required to live a Christian life. There is little in the school curriculum that stresses the conditions and principles for a celebration of life during the different stages of human development. But how is this possible when we have dismantled and eliminated the presence of God in the classroom curriculum in our public schools.

It is possible that a society that eliminates God will eventually succumb to is bestial inclinations to utilize violence as a method of self-expression, pre-mediated offense, or a psychological submission to imitate visual characters extracted from violent video games, movies or to actors using destructive power against their enemies in warfare. There is a fascination with past events that depicted powerful destructive encounters between adversaries who were determined to win the war. Some believe that man's greatest athletic display of physical and psychological energy has been displayed in the countless wars of the past. Men have continued this behavior for the last 5,000 years. It is evident that humans are easily programmed to commit violence if they watch humans being murdered.

It is believed that by the time a teenager reaches the age of 15 years old, he has seen more than 4,000 murders.

So, it is likely that individuals who are suffering from mental problems may search out another dangerous reality using violent actions against others who become the target for their pent-up aggression. When some troubled humans begin to image a "super powerful identity" the next step is to find the opportunity to act out this new portrayal. Consequently, all people of different ages and all social relationships are in danger especially if their usefulness is no longer important or significant.

CHAPTER FIFTEEN

A Third Eye as a Fundamental Step Leading to Intelligence

W E SEEM TO DEFINE THE idea of intelligence with many definitions. Many are open to different interpretations but there is one factor that is ignored, that is fundamental. It involves a natural phenomenon called "movement". It is something that we observe and perform since our infancy. It cannot be ignored since we experience it every day. Humans interact with their environment to survive. Animals move about in search of food and shelter. Birds fly thousands of miles in their migration every year. Humans have created machines and bred animals to carry themselves and goods for centuries. Explorers in the past sought to journey to new continents. Now astronauts are planning to travel to other planets.

All of these human efforts have produced new discoveries and new knowledge. These advances involved the use of an extra sense, a kind of Third Eye to observe and interpret what was happening. The Wright Brothers made many attempts to develop a flying machine but were successful when they discovered that a flexible wing design would get them off the ground. They had to challenge their established mindset and rethink what they are doing. They sought to develop an alternative design thinking. This effort involved considerable self-analysis questioning the existing mindset of the time. This method of thinking opened their minds to think of innovative designs directed at realizing new innovations.

Leonardo da Vinci developed an insatiable appetite to learn about everything, but he soon realized he had to change his perception of what he was viewing. As he began to see things with a different set of spectacles to view phenomena, he was able to attain new insights, new discoveries, new inventions, new artistic depictions. He believed that if you changed your perception, then your mind would produce new information that previously was not apparent.

We seem to have lost this interest in making first-hand observations of our natural phenomena. We rely on accumulated knowledge that only describes animal and human behavior. It doesn't identify the primary factor responsible for this knowledge, the observation of movement. Many of the discoveries in physics were the result of visual observations made of physical entities in particular movements. Newton, Galileo, Einstein and others spent hours observing natural phenomena in order to develop a hypothesis that became an accepted theory.

Children in their infancy learn about the world around them by constantly looking at the movement of the toys in their crib. As they grow, they try to focus and experiment with other things such as household items like pots and pans. When they play in this manner, they begin to understand how to play the game. This ability to change perceptions to see things differently is common among children at play who are not yet conditioned to follow accepted points of view on many topics. They make up scenarios for playing with friends and are apt to change the rules during the play period. This may seem frivolous, but it is a critical aspect of play to explore the unknown or to try new ideas and applications. There is no fear of taking risks and for that reason, their activity can become intense and involve them for hours.

What is interesting is that they spend time observing what the group is doing while at play. They feed off each other's perceptions in visualizing a make-believe scenario or imagined situation. Their play experience becomes very relevant and meaningful. This curiosity and imagination seem to slowly disappear as they become socialized in a school environment that stresses convergent thinking over divergent thinking. The emphasis is not on play but on getting the right answer in the increased testing that is required to evaluate instruction and the content taught. In many ways less emphasis is placed on developing "higher level cognitive functioning" and more on comprehending the increased content that has to be covered. Under these conditions most instruction, the skills and abilities they learn to practice are identified as the lower levels of the Bloom taxonomy. The continued memorization of content while necessary in some of the disciplines becomes the norm and some students lose interest in learning and schooling. They never realize their mental potential as creative "information generators" capable of developing new insights and ideas without having to reference a book… an experience they were accustomed to when they were allowed to crate their learning environment which became relevant and meaningful. This is why many reject the continuous regurgitation of information because their minds are designed to make new connections and discoveries between things that are dissimilar and between ideas that may have a relationship that previously was not evident. This skill and ability is what Benjamin Bloom describes as "SYNERGY at the higher levels in the taxonomy of "Intellectual Skills and Abilities".

There is valid statistical research from a designed study of students using the CORT skills that shows that there are notable statistical increases in more than ten areas in the learning behavior and the verbal discourse between students when they apply the thinking skills developed in the CORT Thinking Skills program by Dr. Edward de Bono, a world-famous author and consultant in developing design thinking. The CORT skills allow students to generate new information that we not previously obvious in the classroom environment.

Reflections/New Insights

THE INTRODUCTION OF INFO-TECH GADGETS has influenced the human mind in ways still unrecognized. Not only have humans become addicted to spending many hours every day texting but they also have become socially isolated from human interaction. This mental transformation has created serious mental problems like loneliness, a fascination with violent behavior, a desire for projecting anormal public images and behavior, and an acceptance of media social-indoctrination as the acceptable platform for understanding the significance of events and important issues. The result is that social/mass media is now the MEDIUM THAT HAS BECOME THE MESSAGE.

This transformation has impacted many institutions that once were the foundations of learning and knowledge. Students in many urban areas are not developing critical cognitive skills necessary to survive in their complex society. Consequently, they can resort to the use of drugs, violent behavior, becoming gang members or radical political groups that seek to undermine established American political beliefs and values. This situation has become more evident in the fact that we seem to be living at a time when America is a divided nation. There is a fierce political war between a radical leftist group that seeks to maintain its power by its affiliation with television personalities that promote the same orchestrated analysis and reactions. We also can listen to opposing television networks that attempt to offer a more objective analysis of issues and current issues.

The future of our republican system of government is in jeopardy because we have not developed the necessary strategies and programs to educate the current generation of Americans who have become indoctrinated by their radicalized teachers and professors who seem interested in promoting their personal political opinions into the fragile/undeveloped minds of their students. Furthermore, we now have recent political leaders who seek to transform American society toward a more socialist one in order to lessen the established freedoms and beliefs. This effort fits well with the beliefs of current globalist leaders who also seek to create a communist state where individual rights are controlled by the government. Current Chinese control of its people is a good example of this intended transformation.

It is obvious to me that we have become victims of our technology that controls our thinking and behavior. I believe this change was noted by world famous Scientist who forewarned us of this transformation. We are not developing the cognitive skills necessary to survive in this new complex millennium. We seem to be trapped in an intelligence trap where our education system has failed our young Americans. The technological revolution has transformed how students think and the unique attitude they have toward information received. They seem to attend to short bits of information as if they were headlines but not always seeking to research what is behind these shortened statements. Consequently, when they read or see televised headlines, they tend to accept them as truth. They depend on these to understand what is happening but now always getting taught. In a similar fashion, they tend to accept what their professors tell them and take courses of study that do little to develop their cognitive skills that are critical in the workplace. Many never develop critical thinking skills. When they enter the workplace, they have difficulty in making decisions, in figuring out problems, and in fulfilling assignments.

The powerful media understands their ability to filter out opinion from the facts. The televised programs are full of opinionated personalities who generalize or present headlines that are in need of validation. The television networks that try to present objective analysis are not capable of exposing the flood of fake news that is communicated on daily basis. The social/mass media continue to bombard viewers with headlines and reports that try to get attention or create controversy. There is an information war to control the minds of Americans who do not have the critical thinking skills to find the truth that will increase their understanding of events and issues impacting their lives.

"WE SEE WITH OUR EYES BUT ONLY
UNDERSTAND USING OUR MINDS"

CONCLUSION
DEVELOPING THE GENIUS MIND

"It is a miracle that the mind completely survives formal education" -Albert Einstein-

THERE ARE SOME WHO BELIEVE that we can use techniques that some of the greatest geniuses used. A researcher, Robert Dillis, studied documents written by Walt Disney, Albert Einstein, and Leonardo da Vinci. He analyzed the writings of these outstanding innovators and described how each of them developed certain methods to accomplish their innovations. In the case of da Vinci, his incredible ability was his technique for seeing more deeply and with greater understanding compared to other observers. Dillis referred to it as *saper vedere* or knowing how to see.

In doing so, da Vinci would be able to work on a problem or idea from many points of view in order to get at its "deepest essence." He would sketch a figure or a scene from many different angles as he did with the painting of The Last Supper. In this instance, he even visited the room at many different times of the day to see the particular effect of light on the wall on which he was painting. In addition to this, da Vinci would brainstorm to enhance his creativity by using "random stimuli" like different stains and paint mixtures until there was a resemblance of views of trees, valleys, plains, mountains, rivers, etc.